BUILDING A NEW WORLD

THE KINGDOMS OF AFRICA

BUILDING A NEW WORLD

AFRICANS IN AMERICA, 1500–1900

PHILIP KOSLOW

CHELSEA HOUSE PUBLISHERS • Philadelphia

Frontispiece: A 19th-century engraving depicting the diamond mines of South Africa.

On the Cover: An artist's interpretation of a bronze head from Benin; in the background, a sugar plantation in the Caribbean.

CHELSEA HOUSE PUBLISHERS
Editorial Director Richard Rennert
Picture Editor Judy Hasday
Art Director Sara Davis
Production Manager Pamela Loos

Staff for BUILDING A NEW WORLD
Senior Editor Jane Shumate
Editorial Assistant Kristine Brennan
Designer Takeshi Takahashi
Picture Researcher Patricia Burns
Cover Illustrator Bradford Brown

First Printing
1 3 5 7 9 8 6 4 2

Library of Congress Cataloging-in-Publication Data

Koslow, Philip.
Building a New World / Philip Koslow
p. cm. — (The kingdoms of Africa)
Includes bibliographical references and index.
Summary: Discusses the ways in which slaves from Africa influenced various aspects of life in the New World, including gold mining, cultivation of sugar and rice, herding live-stock, and ironworking.
ISBN 0-7910-3143-8 (hc)
    0-7910-3144-6 (pbk)
1. America—Civilization—African influences—Juvenile literature. 2. Slavery—America—History—Juvenile literature. [1.Slavery—America—History. 2. America—Civilization—African influences.] I. Title. II. Series
E20.K67 1997   96-45475
970—dc21   CIP
                                        AC

CONTENTS

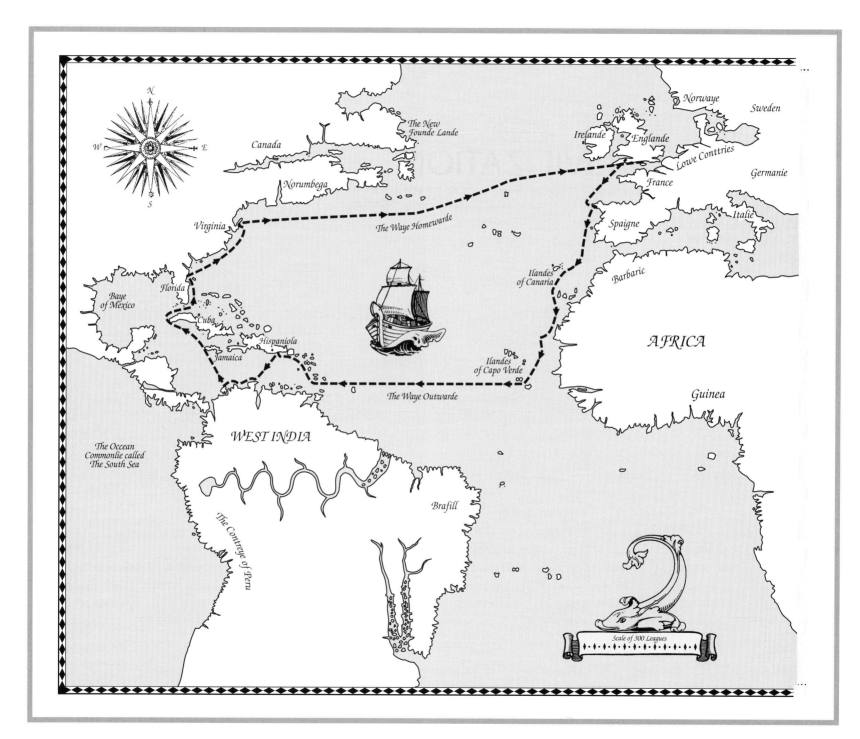

"CIVILIZATION AND MAGNIFICENCE"

On a sunny morning in July 1796, Mungo Park, a Scottish doctor turned explorer, achieved a major goal of his long and difficult trek through West Africa when he reached the banks of the mighty Niger River. Along the river was a cluster of four large towns, which together made up the city of Segu, the principal settlement of the Bambara people. The sight of Segu dazzled Park as much as the spectacle of the broad, shining waterway. "The view of this extensive city," he later wrote, "the numerous canoes upon the river; the crowded population; and the cultivated state of the surrounding country, formed altogether a prospect of civilization and magnificence, which I little expected to find in the bosom of Africa."

On the last leg of his journey, Park encountered a far less happy scene—a caravan of captives being transported from the interior to the coast. There they would be sold to European slave merchants and shipped to the Americas. The unfortunate men and women were shackled together with iron chains and forced to carry heavy loads of provisions on their heads. Having accepted the protection of an African slave merchant, Park traveled with the caravan, which covered more than 25 miles a day across rugged terrain. After nearly six weeks, Park later wrote, they finally reached the coast:

> Although I was now approaching the end of my tedious and toilsome journey; and expected, in another day, to meet with countrymen and friends, I could not part, for the last time, with my unfortunate fellow-travellers, doomed, as I knew most of them

The routes taken by slave ships from Africa across the Atlantic to the Americas became known collectively as the Middle Passage.

7

This engraving shows a European trading center on the African coast, with Portuguese, French, and English compounds erected next to the palace of the local ruler, who is being carried in a sedan chair at the bottom of the picture. Many African rulers supplied European slave traders with captives in exchange for firearms in order to insure their military might.

to be, to a life of captivity and slavery in a foreign land, without great emotion. During a wearisome peregrination of more than five hundred British miles, exposed to the burning rays of a tropical sun, these poor slaves, amid their own infinitely greater sufferings, would commiserate mine; and frequently, of their own accord, bring water to quench my thirst, and at night collect branches and leaves to prepare me a bed in the wilderness. We parted with reciprocal expressions of regret and benediction.

Park returned safely to England, where his book *Travels in the Interior Districts of Africa* became a best-seller. The fate of his companions remains unknown. Some undoubtedly perished on board the crowded, disease-ridden slave ships; others surely died in the New World from brutal exploitation; a few, perhaps, survived their ordeals and founded families that have thrived to this day. It is difficult to trace them because they were deprived of their names along with their freedom. Even their history as a people was swallowed by myths of white racial superiority. Only a century after Park published his unbiased views, for example, a professor at Britain's Oxford University stated that African history before the coming of Europeans had been nothing more than "blank, uninteresting, brutal barbarism."

Inevitably, views such as these put down powerful roots in the Americas. They were echoed by leading scholars such as Ulrich B. Phillips, a pioneer in the study of U.S. slavery, who wrote in 1918 that plantation life had enabled Africans to make "slow progress from barbarism to civilization." In the view of Phillips and countless others, all successful ventures in the Americas were the work of white Europeans and their descendants. Africans, allegedly lacking any real

9

African slave traders march a caravan of captives across the savanna to the coast, where they will be sold to Europeans. Of all the captives taken in the interior of Africa, only about one-third reached the New World; most perished during the harsh overland journey or in the suffocating holds of slave ships.

history or achievements of their own, had contributed nothing but unreasoning muscle power.

These beliefs finally began to crumble after the end of World War II in 1945. At that time, the African continent began to free itself from European domination, and scholars from many nations began intensive studies of African history. Little by little, centuries-old misconceptions have given way to an understanding of Africa's crucial role in world history.

Human history begins in Africa: about 7.5 million years ago, the first humanlike creatures, known as hominids, appeared on the African continent and gradually evolved into *Homo sapiens*, the species to which all modern humans belong. From

Africa, *Homo sapiens* began to populate the rest of the world about 150,000 years ago. Thus, present-day peoples of all races and nationalities share a common heritage—and that heritage is decidedly African.

In addition, Africans were the first tool makers. In 1995, a collection of objects carved from the bones of large mammals, including barbed spear points and cutting blades, was unearthed in the central African nation of Zaire. Using various technologies to determine the age of these objects, scientists concluded that they were between 75,000 and 90,000 years old. Similar tools discovered in Europe have been found to be only 14,000 years old.

Building on their early accomplishments, Africans developed a host of sophisticated civilizations, beginning with the so-called Nok culture, which flourished in central Nigeria as early as the 5th century B.C., and ending with such kingdoms as Benin and Asante, which endured until the beginning of the 20th century. The saga of African achievement was interrupted only by the growth of the transatlantic slave trade, which disrupted African societies while producing fabulous wealth for Europe. Between 1500 and 1900, at least 12 million Africans were transported to the Americas, constituting the largest migration in human history. Given the richness of their past, it was inevitable that these men and women, with their age-old skills, would play a vital and creative role in the building of a new world.

Chapter 1 | RICHES AND REBELLION

This fanciful engraving by the French artist Jean Strudan depicts the explorer Christopher Columbus on the bridge of his ship as he approaches the New World. Columbus's 1492 voyage to the Caribbean paved the way for the European conquest of the Americas—and the forced migration of millions of Africans to the New World.

Thousands of years before Christopher Columbus landed on Hispaniola (now Haiti and the Dominican Republic) and claimed that he had discovered a new world, various peoples had migrated to the continent from Asia and had inhabited the lands ever since. Columbus was not even the first European to set foot in the Americas; more than 400 years before his arrival, Norsemen visited present-day Newfoundland, Canada, in their Viking ships, establishing small settlements that they soon abandoned. A handful of scholars have also suggested that groups of West Africans sailed to the Americas 40 to 50 years ahead of Columbus, though this view has been hotly debated.

Columbus has retained one distinction, though—he was almost certainly the first European to bring an African to the New World. The ship's register for Columbus's third voyage to the Americas, which took place in 1498, listed "Diego el Negro," a West African slave who had been living in Spain as a personal servant. And four years later, when the Spanish crown named Nicolás de Ovando the first governor of Hispaniola, he was accompanied on his journey by several black servants.

The first sizable shipment of African slaves to the Caribbean, however, took place in 1517. These individuals made their presence felt immediately. As the Spaniards spread their power throughout the Caribbean and into North and South America, a number of Africans took part in their military campaigns and explorations. Most notably, Africans

13

14

participated in Vasco Núñez de Balboa's expedition to the Pacific Ocean in 1513 and in Francisco Pizarro's conquest of Peru during the 1520s.

The individual deeds of these African soldiers and explorers were not usually recorded in the Spanish chronicles of that brutal, swashbuckling era. One notable exception was a Moroccan slave named Estevanico, who was a crucial translator and advance scout for Cabeza de Vaca and later Spanish explorers in America's Southwest. Another exception was Juan Valiente, a slave who fled his owner in Mexico and joined the Spanish forces in Chile. Beginning as a common soldier, Valiente so distinguished himself in battles with the Indians that he was promoted to the rank of captain and even received a parcel of land and a group of Indian slaves to help him work it. Though Valiente's attempt to purchase his freedom was thwarted by his vengeful owner, his son managed to inherit his property and live as a free man.

At first, the Spaniards looked to the conquered Native Americans for the workers they needed to build a New World empire on the Caribbean islands and in the Americas. The Spaniards saw that the climate was excellent for crops popular in Europe, such as coffee, cotton, sugar, and tobacco; they were also convinced that these lands were full of gold and silver. The Native Americans they had encountered—or Indians, as the Spaniards called them—were, according to Columbus himself, "naked and defenseless, hence ready to be given orders and put to work" cultivating and mining the land.

However, the Spanish soon encountered problems. In many cases, the Indians, accustomed to hunting and farming small plots of land, could not withstand the heavy labor demanded of them. They also had no natural resistance to European diseases such as smallpox and typhus and so began to die by the thousands. Before long, the native populations of Caribbean islands such as Hispaniola were completely eradicated. The sufferings of the Indians soon aroused the compassion of the Catholic church; at the urging of the clergy, the Spanish monarchy banned

This cross-section of Potosí by the Dutch artist Theodore de Bry shows miners extracting silver from the legendary mountain. African and Indian slaves working the mines of South America were not likely to survive more than a few years on the job, but those who did sometimes earned enough money to buy their freedom.

Indian slavery in the Americas in 1542. Though Indians continued to toil for Spaniards, they did so under the official status of hired laborers.

The Spanish clergy had no objection to the enslavement of Africans to provide labor for the New World, however. Consequently, the slave trade soon flourished among Africa, Europe, and the Americas, and the numbers of African slaves quickly increased throughout the Spanish dominions, as well as in the vast territory of Brazil, which Spain had ceded to the Portuguese in 1494. As they arrived, the African slaves began working at various tasks, including the cultivation of sugar and tobacco. Initially, though, there was nothing the Spaniards coveted more than gold and silver, and in this quest for riches Africans played a decisive role.

Africans had been mining gold for centuries. Black Africa's first great kingdom, ancient Ghana, which began to flourish around 750, grew rich by regulating the gold trade between North African merchants and the miners of Bambuk, sheltered deep in the coastal forest belt. When ancient Ghana declined during the 12th century, the riches of Bambuk were exploited by the even greater empires of Mali and Songhay, both of which drew upon the wealth of additional goldfields at nearby Bure. During the 18th and 19th centuries, the Akan goldfields, located in the valley of the Volta River, emerged as the richest of all, supporting the glittering kingdom of Asante.

Because African miners did not have draft animals or water-powered wheels to help them dig shafts or clear mines of water and debris, mining in Africa required a huge human labor force. In Asante, miners were normally slaves captured in wars against neighboring peoples, and the laws of the nation even forbade citizens to work in the mines. These mining operations were well known to the European seamen and merchants who began to visit the African coast during the 15th century. After Spanish explorers discovered gold and silver in the Americas during the 1540s, they quickly began importing even more captive Africans to the mining regions of the New World.

The most famous of all the American mines was located on the great mountain of Potosí, in the present-day nation of Bolivia. Potosí produced such fabulous amounts of silver that Spanish speakers still say "Vale un Potosí" to mean "It's worth a fortune." African

(Continued on page 21)

16

BRILLIANCE IN METAL

Many of the Africans transported to the Americas came from cultures famed for their skill in mining and metalwork. Ancient Ghana, for instance, had controlled a vast gold trade in the 11th century, while nearby Benin reached its peak in the early 1500s, when sculptors filled the royal palace with bronze plaques. Among many West African peoples, works of art were produced by blacksmiths, who created both ordinary utensils and sacred objects; their skills would be exhibited again in the metalwork of the New World.

A wrought-iron equestrian figure that may represent the mythical blacksmith who brought fire and metallurgy to the people of Mali.

Brass leopard from Benin. The leopard is featured in many Benin artworks as it is closely associated with one of the country's most powerful rulers of the 15th century.

Brass anklets crafted by the Igbo people in the Niger region.

19

This 16th-century bronze plaque, which decorated the royal palace in Benin, depicts part of a ritual evoking a legendary war against the sky.

(Continued from page 16)

slaves were always outnumbered by Indian laborers at Potosí and the silver mines of Mexico, amounting at most to 16 percent of the work force. But Spanish records show that colonial officials continually requested more African slaves, indicating that the Spaniards considered Africans essential to the operation of the mines. For this reason, Africans were granted special privileges denied the Indians, such as the right to carry weapons and to wear European clothing.

Being earmarked for mine work in the New World was hardly an enviable fate, however. Gold mines were usually situated in sweltering valleys, while silver mines, like the one on Potosí, were in bleak highlands where the air was thin and ice cold. Miners typically worked from dawn to dusk, and officials estimated a miner's average working life at 6 to 8 years; even the hardiest individuals rarely survived more than 12.

In Brazil, slaves commonly panned for gold in streams and rivers, bending over for hours with their legs or even the entire lower halves of their bodies underwater; youngsters performing this work often had their growth stunted, and many miners became grotesquely bowlegged or otherwise deformed. In addition, the contrast in temperature between the frigid water and the sweltering air brought on dangerous ailments, such as kidney disease, pleurisy, and pneumonia.

Even with all these dangers, Africans generally preferred mining to plantation work. Miners were allowed more freedom of movement, received rations of tobacco and brandy, and often had opportunities to enrich themselves. Any slave finding an especially valuable nugget was given a reward, and mine owners often allowed slaves to prospect on their own once they had met a certain quota. Moreover, even the most vigilant overseer could not prevent workers from taking small amounts of precious material for themselves; slaves who worked in Brazil's diamond mines were especially adept at hiding small gems under their nails or in the webbing between their fingers and toes. By such means, many mine workers purchased their freedom. Some migrated to the cities, where they entered new crafts and trades; but many remained in the mining districts and continued to work as independent prospectors.

In the British colonies of eastern North America, there were few deposits of precious metals, so mining did not

African slaves engage in capoeira *in 19th-century Brazil. Capoeira remains a vital tradition in Afro-Brazilian culture and is linked to the legend of Zumbi, Brazil's greatest African freedom fighter during the 17th century.*

valuable commodities, such as coal, salt, lead, and iron ore. When the United States came into being in the late 18th century, the new nation's growing industries depended mainly on coal from eastern Virginia. Visiting a Virginia mine in 1796, a French nobleman noted that the owners knew virtually nothing about mining and depended on their 500 black slaves to make the venture work. The same observations were made by visitors to other locations over the years and confirmed by a mine operator who declared in 1859, "I have not a white man on my work. . . . I must have a negro force or give up my business." In many U.S. mines, African Americans served as foremen and also functioned as highly skilled machinists, black-smiths, and carpenters.

Despite the slight prestige or opportunities African mine workers gained, however, they were still slaves. They were subjected to a grinding routine of heavy labor, frequently in the dark, in poorly ventilated tunnels, and exposed to the dangers of cave-ins, floods, fires, and explosions. Often, along with other slaves, they escaped or revolted against those who kept them in bondage. The hard labor and specialized skills of African slaves helped build the physical

occupy the African slaves who began arriving there in 1619. Later generations of African Americans, however, played a leading role in the extraction of other

landscape of the New World, but their continuing struggle for freedom was crucial to shaping its culture.

In 17th-century Brazil, for example, escaped slaves made a bold attempt to recapture their African heritage by creating the kingdom of Palmares. At its height, Palmares extended over 1,200 square miles in eastern Brazil and contained some 20,000 inhabitants. The kingdom's greatest leader was Zumbi, an African Brazilian who had been born into slavery in 1655. After fleeing to Palmares at the age of 15, Zumbi became a military commander and finally the nation's ruler after deposing his uncle, who was trying to negotiate a treaty with Brazil's Portuguese overlords.

The existence of Palmares was a direct threat to Portuguese control over Brazil's slave population, and beginning in 1670 the Portuguese mounted yearly attacks on the African state. Palmares's settlements were fortified with palisades of sharpened wooden stakes, a technique commonly used in Africa, and the defenders held out against Portuguese troops for 25 years. Finally, in 1694, the Portuguese governor mounted an all-out assault that included Indian scouts and specialized slave hunters brought from other regions. After 42 days of fighting, the attackers broke through the defenses of Palmares and destroyed the kingdom. Zumbi himself escaped with a small band of followers and continued to fight the Portuguese for 18 more months until he was finally captured and executed.

In modern-day Brazil, Zumbi has become a legendary hero to the many Brazilians of African descent, who form the largest black community in the world outside Africa. Numerous neighborhoods, businesses, and musical groups have adopted Zumbi's name, and he is also taken as a role model by schools that teach *capoeira*, a dance-based version of the martial arts. Most significantly, Zumbi also plays a prominent role in the religion known as Umbanda, which combines many traditional African beliefs with Roman Catholicism. The adherents of Umbanda make regular pilgrimages to Palmares. Dressed in white from head to toe, the pilgrims gather beneath the trees that have overgrown the vanished fortifications of the once-great African kingdom; in the flickering light of votive candles, they leave offerings of flowers and food to the spirits of those long-departed warriors who blazed the trail of freedom in the Americas.

Chapter 2 | PLANTING THE SUGAR FIELDS

Brazilian men use a hand-cranked press to extract the juice from sugar cane. As large sugar plantations sprang up in the southern United States during the 18th and 19th centuries, the demand for skilled slave labor increased.

In the United States, the word *slavery* often evokes images of the great cotton plantations of the antebellum (pre–Civil War) South, and with good reason. According to census figures compiled in 1850, 2.5 million U.S. slaves were employed in agriculture; out of these, 1.85 million cultivated cotton. However, the history of the plantation goes a great deal farther back in history.

The plantation system dates back to the 13th century, when Europeans grew sugarcane (derived originally from India) on large estates on the island of Cyprus in the Mediterranean Sea. When Portuguese seamen and merchants began exploring the West African coast during the 15th century, they soon realized that offshore islands such as São Tomé and Principe were ideal for sugar culti-

vation. The Portuguese created sugar plantations on these islands and manned them with slaves purchased from African rulers. As the Portuguese and Spanish established themselves in the New World, they immediately recognized the immense potential for sugar production in the Caribbean islands and the warmer regions of the South American continent.

Though Africans had not cultivated sugar in their homelands, they were accustomed to the sweltering climate of the sugar colonies and to the work involved in creating plantations. The first requirement of growing sugar was clearing large tracts of land, and in this endeavor Africans had far more experience than Europeans. Europe's fertile farmlands had long before been cleared and settled. In Africa, especially in the coastal forest regions, residents were constantly hacking away dense vegetation to establish new communities and plant crops. In addition to cutting trees and undergrowth with axes and machetes, they also cleared land by setting carefully controlled fires, later using the ashes as fertilizer.

Africans were also highly skilled at growing delicate crops in tropical soil, and they had long experience of large-scale collective labor. In almost every African community, citizens worked together to clear fields, put up defensive walls, and build houses. This tradition was perhaps most highly developed in Dahomey, one of the principal sources of New World slaves. All able-bodied Dahomean men were required to join a village group called the *dokpwe*, which performed essential tasks for the benefit of the community. Anyone who shirked this duty was liable to be disowned by his village and his family.

The New World sugar growers quickly noticed Africans' agricultural skills, and the tide of slaves shipped from Africa surged into the millions. Of the 12 million African slaves who entered the Americas between 1450 and 1870, an estimated three-quarters were employed on sugar plantations. By the 18th century—when Spain was in decline and England, France, and Holland were the dominant colonial powers in the Americas—sugar was the most important commodity in the world economy.

Factories in European cities such as Liverpool, England, produced the goods—textiles, glassware, cutlery, and firearms—that were traded for slaves in Africa. When African slaves were transported to the New World, they were exchanged for sugar, molasses, and other agricultural products, which were then sold at great profit in Europe. This Triangle Trade, as it became known, made Europe the center of the world economy—and the Triangle Trade was driven by the labor of Africans toiling on the sugar plantations of the Americas. (Only at the very end of the century, when the cotton gin was invented, did cotton begin to rival and replace sugar as the main transatlantic commodity.)

On sugar plantations, slaves worked six days a week throughout the entire year. Typically, the workers plowed and hoed the fields throughout the winter months and planted the seed cane in early spring. During the spring and summer they tended the growing shoots, until the cane was fully grown.

In this woodcut of a Louisiana sugar plantation, field hands harvest sugarcane (right), while other workers haul the cane stalks to the mill (left). By 1850, 2.5 million African slaves were working on plantations producing sugar, rice, cotton, and other crops.

27

From October until the end of the year, the slaves worked at a frantic pace. They cut and gathered the cane and then hauled it to the mill, where it was ground and boiled. When the cane juice cooled, the sugar crystals were drawn off and packed into barrels (known as hogsheads) for shipping.

The workday on a typical sugar plantation—and also on plantations producing tobacco, indigo, coffee, cotton, and rice—was highly regimented. Well before the sun came up, slaves were roused by the blowing of a horn or a conch shell. All were expected to be in the fields and ready to work at the first glimmer of daylight. There was a break for breakfast around seven o'clock and another break for lunch at noontime. During the hottest weather, the slaves would often be allowed to rest for two or three hours in the middle of the day and then resume working until the late evening. If the overseer saw fit, they would sometimes work into the night with the aid of moonlight or torches.

Plantation labor throughout the New World was organized on two distinct patterns: the task system and the gang system. Under the task system, laborers would be given a specific amount of work to do; as soon as the target was reached, slaves were free to do as they wished and would sometimes be offered pay for extra work. Under the gang system, all slaves worked in unison at a single task for the full length of the workday.

Not surprisingly, most slaves preferred the task system. Tasks were often tailored to age and capacity: teenagers would be asked to perform three-quarters of the task, younger boys and girls one-half, and children one-fourth. Those who did their work quickly and efficiently could often leave the field in the middle of the afternoon and have the rest of the day to themselves. Some planters considered it dangerous to provide their slaves with leisure time, while others found that tasking encouraged them to work more efficiently. In practice, planters often used both systems at once. Plowing was commonly done by gangs, whereas hoeing was often handled through the task system, with each hand assigned to cultivate a specific part of the field, usually a quarter acre.

Though field work was the mainstay of plantation life, slaves were also involved in many complex tasks. Blacksmiths repaired tools; carpenters erected houses, barns, and work sheds; coopers made barrels; hostlers cared for animals; teamsters hauled crops and equipment; and machinists operated sugar grinders, boilers, cotton gins, steam engines, and other essential pieces of equipment.

On sugar plantations, the sugar boiler was a master craftsman who had to possess a vast knowledge of soils, cane types, growing conditions, and harvesting techniques; the grindings from each type of cane had to be processed in a particular manner to yield the best sugar crystals. Plantation owners often recruited their sugar boilers from Africans of the inland savanna regions; taller and thinner than the average, they were believed better able to bend for hours above the steaming

sugar vats. The most desired field hands, by contrast, were the shorter, stockier peoples from Africa's coastal regions, especially the yam-growing areas bordering the Bight of Benin.

The plantation system was designed purely to exploit the labor of slaves, with

African rebels on the Caribbean island of St. Domingue battle French troops in 1802. After fighting the powerful French forces to a standstill, the Africans secured their freedom and founded Haiti, the second independent nation in the Americas (the first being the United States).

TOUSSAINT L'OUVERTURE

reçoit une Lettre du premier Consul.

little regard for the human cost involved. Work on sugar plantations took the greatest human toll, as the health of countless slaves was broken by endless hours of cutting cane under a broiling sun or breathing the dense fumes that rose from the boiling vats. A British visitor to an 18th-century sugar plantation in the Dutch colony of Surinam estimated that "the whole race of healthy slaves, consisting of 50,000, are totally extinct once every twenty years." Those who perished were replaced by thousands more from Africa.

African slaves on plantations in the early colonial days of North America, on the other hand, were not much worse off than white indentured servants—European immigrants who had agreed to work in bondage for a set amount of time in exchange for the cost of their passage to America. Like indentured servants in the early 1600s, African slaves working on tobacco plantations in Virginia, for example, might ultimate-

François Dominique Toussaint L'Ouverture (1744-1803) led the slave revolts that ended English and French control over the island of St. Domingue. Hailed as one of the greatest men of the age—even by his opponents—Toussaint excelled as both a military commander and political organizer.

ly gain their freedom, purchasing it or even arguing for it in the law courts. This fairly equal treatment of white and black bonded laborers in the American colonies did not last long, however; by the end of the 17th century, the practice of indentured servitude had dropped off, and enslavement of Africans had become a widespread and entrenched institution. The treatment of black slaves would worsen considerably in the years to come.

Some planters, more humane or merely more sensible than the rest, realized that they could get better work out of their slaves by providing liberties and incentives rather than relying on physical force. In these places, plantation slaves were encouraged to raise crops on their own plots of land and to sell their produce. On Antigua, in the Caribbean, the entire populace came to depend on these markets; European visitors noted that the islands' whites would have starved if not for the provisions grown by the slaves.

Africans and African Americans in bondage made numerous efforts to assert their humanity and independence. Like the African Brazilians who founded Palmares, slaves throughout the Americas continued to resist. Many escaped from the plantations and later helped others do the same. Others channeled their rage into violent rebellion; in the 1700s there were at least 250 slave revolts of varying force. And in 1791, Toussaint L'Ouverture led a slave rebellion in the French colony of Saint-Domingue and spurred the creation of Haiti, the first independent black nation in the West.

Chapter 3 | RICE GROWERS

A view of a rice field along the Savannah River, which flows between South Carolina and Georgia. Thanks to native African expertise, rice became a staple crop in the first colonies of the southeastern states. Note the watercourse that runs through this field for controlled flooding (center left).

When a shipload of settlers from the Caribbean island of Barbados established a new British colony in South Carolina in 1670, an African was in their party. Three of his countrymen followed on a second ship a week later. The African influx increased steadily as the colony grew, and during Carolina's early years no less than one-fourth of the inhabitants were black. Those who had lived in the coastal regions of West Africa were especially valued for their expertise in boat building, diving, fishing, and navigating coastal waters and swamps; natives of the savanna, on the other hand, were prized for their skill with cattle and horses.

In addition to raising cattle, the Carolina colonists tried their hand at growing olives, cotton, indigo, grapes, and tobacco. They had no thought at first of cultivating rice as a major crop. Yet by 1720 rice had become the colonists' most important food item, and by 1750 it was South Carolina's major export. This change took place during a time when the black population of Carolina steadily grew to exceed the colony's white population. It was no mere coincidence that rice culture grew with the influx of Africans.

Although rice—originally an Asian crop—had been grown by southern Italians since the 15th century, northern Europeans, whose native climate and geography are not suitable for rice culture, had little knowledge of the crop, even in the 18th century. African farmers, however, had long been growing rice on the West Atlantic coast and along the

A wooden mortar and pestle, used to separate the rice grains from their husks. Common throughout the southern rice country, these tools were traditional African implements. The mortar was usually fashioned by hollowing out part of the trunk of a pine, cypress, or gum tree.

34

middle Niger, where the river floods during the rainy season and creates a vast inland delta. Again, the specialized knowledge of certain African groups would be crucial to the development of the American continents.

When the British attempted to establish a settlement in eastern Florida, for example, one of the men involved wrote, "I . . . must choose [Africans] such as are used to the difficult Cultivations I begin with as Rice, Cotton, Indigo, etc." Similarly, when early French colonists in

Louisiana found themselves on the verge of starvation, the officials in charge sent out a request for African cultivators. One ship's captain bound for Africa was given the following instructions: "In the different places where the said Sieur Herpin trades negroes he will manage to trade for a few who know how to cultivate rice. He will also trade for three or four hogsheads of rice suitable for planting, which he will deliver to the directors of the Company on his arrival in the colony."

During the 18th century, the African regions along the Atlantic coast provided 43 percent of South Carolina's African immigrants. Africans who found themselves on the sea islands and in the coastal lowlands of Carolina would have encountered familiar terrain well suited to growing rice. Their experience was crucial to the success of rice cultivation, a difficult and complex process requiring great care and precise timing.

During the winter months, the slaves were occupied in building the intricate series of ditches, dams, and watercourses that allowed them to regulate the flow of ocean and river tides. The actual growing season began in the middle of March and extended to the end of August. First the rice seeds were planted in long furrows. Then the floodgates surrounding the fields were opened, allowing water to fill the furrows and germinate the seeds. After five days, the water was allowed to drain off, and the ground was left to dry. When the rice had risen to a few inches, the fields were flooded again in order to kill the grass and weeds. In the middle of May, the water was drawn off again, and the fields remained dry for two months; at this point, the hands were constantly working with hoes, uprooting weeds and loosening the soil around the plants. Finally, in the middle of July, the fields were flooded for a third time, and the rice was allowed to ripen on its own.

Charles Ball, a Mississippi slave who passed through South Carolina in his travels, described a rice field in his book *Fifty Years in Chains*: "The rice was nearly two feet in height above the water, and of a vivid green color, covering a large space, of at least a hundred acres. Had it not been for the water, which appeared stagnant and sickly, and swarmed with frogs and thousands of snakes, it would have been as fine a sight as one need wish to look on."

In addition to concealing snakes and frogs, the waters of the rice fields bred swarms of mosquitoes, some of which carried the deadly malaria parasite. Though many workers from the coastal regions of Africa had inherited a partial immunity to malaria, they still fell ill at an alarming rate. Basil Hall, a captain in the British Navy who visited a Carolina plantation in the 1820s, made the following observation:

An African-American slave pounds rice with a mortar and pestle. In some parts of the South, African Americans still cultivate rice using the methods of their ancestors.

The cultivation of rice was described to me as by far the most unhealthy work in which the slaves were employed; and, in spite of every care, that they sank under it in great numbers. The causes of this dreadful mortality, are the constant moisture and heat of the atmosphere, together with the alternate floodings and dryings of the fields, on which the negroes are perpetually at work, often ankle-deep in mud, with their bare heads exposed to the fierce rays of the sun. At such season every white man leaves the spot as a matter of course, and proceeds inland to the high grounds; or, if he can afford it, he travels northward to the springs of Saratoga, or the Lakes of Canada.

Despite these punishing conditions, enough workers always survived to bring in the yearly rice harvest, which extended from the end of August into October. At this time, the men would cut the tall stalks of rice with crescent-bladed knives, and the women would gather the cut stalks and tie them into bundles. When all the crop was in, the slaves would thresh the rice, beating the pods off the stalks with long sticks known as flails. They would then pour the pods into large wooden mortars (fashioned from tree trunks) and separate the grains from the husks by pounding them with hand-carved wooden pestles.

Having observed the entire cultivation process as well as the other work done around the plantation, Captain Hall gained a deep appreciation for the ability of the African-American workers. He was especially impressed with a blacksmith named Caesar, who deftly performed a complicated repair job on one of Hall's possessions:

The rest of the party having walked on, I staid to have some conversation with Caesar, whose correct acquaintance not only with his own mechanical operations, but with many other things, surprised me a good deal, and I left the smithy, with my opinion of the whole black race raised in the scale by this trivial incident. Of such flimsy materials is prejudice built! . . . I think it right to mention, that as far as my own experience has gone, I have invariably noticed that precisely in proportion as the negro has a fair chance given him, so he proves himself equal in capacity to the white man.

Perhaps because of the rapid increase in the South's black population—it reached nearly 4 million in the 1850s—white southerners became more and more eager to deny the slaves' capa-

(Continued on page 41)

NEW WORLD SCENES

Fascinated by the "New World," European artists recorded—and romanticized—what they saw, as the mountains and fields of the Caribbean and Americas were explored, exploited, and transformed through the labor of millions of Africans.

This page from the Histoire Naturelles des Indes, *written in French in the 16th century, portrays a furnace used to smelt silver.*

A romanticized scene of slaves enjoying tropical fruits, sugarcane, and rum outside their house in Martinique, where they would probably have worked a backbreaking day in the sugarfields. The painting was done by Le Masurier in 1775.

Augustin Brunais's depiction of a marketplace with a linen stall and a vegetable seller in a South American colonial settlement.

*Slaves wash for diamonds under
the watchful eyes of their overseers
in Brazil in this 1815 illustration.*

(Continued from page 36)

bilities and to maintain the separation of the races. One of their prime weapons was the argument that African Americans were biologically inferior to whites and thus naturally fitted for servitude. This had not been the general view during the early years of the southern colonies, when Africans had often worked side by side with white indentured servants. But the myth of white superiority finally came to rule the South—which depended, after all, on slave labor—and this idea held sway in many parts of the nation long after slavery was abolished.

Despite enduring prejudice and injustice, later generations of black Carolinians held on to elements of their tradition, including the rice-growing talent of their ancestors. The survival of these skills was documented by Amelia Watson Vernon, a native of Mars Bluff, South Carolina. Mars Bluff, upland terrain some 65 miles from the coast, had always been cotton country, and rice had played no part in its economy over the years. Yet despite the region's unsuitability for the crop, Mars Bluff's African Americans had cultivated rice on small plots of land right through the early years of the 20th century. Some had laid out their rice fields in hollows

that filled with rainwater; others had built ingenious irrigation systems to create the proper conditions for the sprouting of the seeds. The local method of pounding rice grains in a mortar and pestle was distinctively African in origin and had been passed from generation to generation in South Carolina.

According to Vernon, Joseph Opala, an anthropologist who had researched rice growing in Africa, offered an explanation as to why people had expended so much labor, after working their regular jobs, to cultivate these modest rice fields:

> Rice growers everywhere felt a pride in their skill. It gave them status. . . . Opala thought that sense of status might explain why some Mars Bluff African Americans continued planting their small fields of rice into the 1920s, when there was apparently no merchant to buy their crop. . . . That skill had set them apart as special, and it had given them a degree of autonomy when autonomy was a hard thing for an African American to find.

41

Chapter 4 | RIDING THE RANGE

This engraving depicts a mounted warrior in the employ of Sheikh Muhammad al-Kanemi, the 19th-century ruler of Borno in West Africa. Horsemanship was a decisive factor in the history of many African kingdoms: mounted cavalry forces enabled ambitious rulers to conquer large territories in the creation of vast empires.

As Europeans were establishing their colonies in the New World, one of their primary needs was for livestock—cattle and pigs for food, and horses and mules for transportation and plowing. In Europe, where land was scarce, farm animals were normally kept in pastures and slaughtered annually except for a handful selected for breeding. In the New World, however, land was plentiful. European settlers found that open grazing was the most suitable means of raising livestock, and this required slaughtering only those animals absolutely needed for food. However, Europeans were not accustomed to tending large herds of animals on open land, nor were Native Americans, most of whom subsisted either on a vegetable diet or by hunting wild game. The void in expertise was filled by Africans.

Not all Africans were adept at handling livestock. In the forest regions of West Africa, the inhabitants could not raise cattle and horses due to the presence of the tsetse fly, which transmits the fatal disease known as sleeping sickness to both humans and animals. But the tsetse does not breed in the grasslands and open woodlands of the savanna. In those areas Africans have been raising cattle since at least 4000 B.C. and horses since 500 B.C.

The most notable cattle herders of West Africa were (and still are) the tall, slender, copper-skinned Fulani, who originated in the southern fringes of the Sahara about A.D. 1000 and gradually spread throughout the savanna as they sought pasturage for their herds of cat-

Herders tend their cattle near a village in the African republic of Niger in the late 1960s. In the West African savanna, which stretches from the Atlantic Ocean to the Nile Valley, black Africans have been raising livestock for more than 6,000 years.

44

tle. The Fulani language, known as Fulfulde, contains numerous words for "cattle," each word describing a particular breed or coloration. *Felle baleye,* for example, means "black with a white star"; *amare* means "white with red flanks"; *nore* denotes a red steer with a white stripe along its back. Other words describe animals by the distinctive twist of their horns. Armed with such sophisticated knowledge, the typical Fulani nomad knows each member of his herd and is always aware when one is missing. When moving his beasts, the herder is constantly crying out, addressing individual animals with the words that denote their physical type.

Horses had played a significant role in the development of West African kingdoms since the emergence of ancient Ghana. Indeed, most of the great savanna kingdoms—Mali, Songhay, Kanem-Borno, Nupe, the Hausa states, and Oyo, among others—had been founded by groups of mounted warriors. These horse soldiers had in many cases broken away from established kingdoms and were often led by princes who were barred from inheriting the throne by older brothers or other rivals. Typically, the warriors would invade a region where people lived in scattered farming villages. After ousting the village chiefs, the horsemen would install themselves as rulers, marrying local women and often forming new ethnic groups with distinctive languages. Throughout the history of these states, the possession of horses remained a key to power. Some kingdoms were renowned for their armored cavalry as late as the 19th century, and equestrian displays still play a major role in the traditional celebrations of many West African peoples, especially in northern Nigeria.

The early slave traders were well aware of Africans' skill with domestic animals. Just as New World mine operators sought Africans from the areas bordering the Bight of Benin, where mining was a common activity, colonial officials wishing to raise livestock often requested slaves from Senegambia, on the west coast. Senegambian peoples included not only Fulani but also many others skilled in horsemanship and animal husbandry, such as Wolof, Serer, and Mandingo. Nupe from northern Nigeria were also highly desired as cattle hands.

Under the care of these seasoned herders, the cattle stock of colonies such as South Carolina grew at a spectacular pace. By 1710, just 40 years after the introduction of cattle, the average Carolinian settler had seen his herd grow from 3 or 4 beasts to 200 or more, and some herds had grown beyond 1,000. Similarly, the great cattle herds of the Caribbean islands and the South American mainland were often placed in the care of West Africans. In 1818, an English traveler in Argentina reported that one ranch proprietor owned 60,000 head of cattle and employed 80 black cowboys to watch over them.

Some of these black cowhands joined the ranks of the legendary gauchos who ruled the great Argentinean pampas. These swashbuckling charac- ters—of Spanish and Indian blood as well as African—housed their families in crude mud huts, made their own boots and saddles from the hides of slaughtered cattle, and virtually lived on horseback as they pursued their rugged, independent way of life. They also developed their tracking and pathfinding skills to a nearly superhuman level. It was said that a gaucho could follow a trail that was two years old or identify the hoof prints of a missing horse among the tracks of an entire herd. He could find his way on a moonless night simply by smelling the earth and could tell from a cloud of dust on the horizon how many men or animals were approaching. Among the gauchos, these skills—as well as strength, endurance, and a willingness to fight to the death for personal honor—were far more important than skin color.

Akin to the gauchos on the Argentinean pampas were the frontiersmen in the American West. In the early 1800s, the new United States was pushing westward, following the trails blazed by fur trappers, gold miners, and settlers. African Americans were among these frontiersmen, and one of the best known was James Beckwourth, born the son of a plantation master and a slave around

African-American cavalryman in action during the 1890s, as depicted by Frederick Remington. Known as the Buffalo Soldiers, members of the all-black 9th and 10th U.S. Cavalry were nicknamed by Native Americans, who likened the texture of their hair—and their courage—to that of the revered buffalo.

46

1800. Although legally a slave, he was treated as a son by his white father, who sent him to school and also encouraged his love of the wild. By the time Beckwourth reached his early 20s, he had grown tired of his career of blacksmithing and set out to become a fur trapper in the Rocky Mountains—and to lead one of the most independent lives imaginable. He blazed trails across the Sierra Nevada, fought the Seminole Indians in Florida, became a Crow Indian war chief, and served as a U.S. Army cavalry guide in Colorado. At a time when most black Americans enjoyed few liberties, Beckwourth roamed far and free. He died the year after the Civil War—and the slavery of black Americans—ended, in 1866.

Some of the 180,000 African Americans who had fought in the victorious Union army during the Civil War formed two new black mounted regiments, the 9th and 10th Cavalry. Popularly known as the Buffalo Soldiers, these intrepid warriors played a pivotal role in claiming the West and later distinguished themselves during the Spanish-American War in 1898. Other adventurous African Americans went west to seek their fortune as cowpunchers: in the 1870s and 1880s, some 5,000 black drovers proved their mettle on the famed Chisholm Trail, where they helped drive huge herds of longhorn steers from San Antonio, Texas, up to Abilene, Kansas. Among those who earned a place in the legends of the West were Nat Love, Bronco Sam, Bill Pickett, One Horse Charley, George Glenn, and Bose Ikard. Though less well known than white western legends such as Wild Bill Hickok, Buffalo Bill Cody, and Wyatt Earp, these men were no less respected and feared in the rugged world of the American frontier.

Love, otherwise known as Deadwood Dick, had been born into slavery on a tobacco plantation in Tennessee in 1854. After emancipation, he hired himself out as a farm laborer and began breaking in colts as a sideline, earning 10 cents for each animal he tamed. Realizing that he had an unusual talent with horses, Love left home at the age of 15 and arrived in the wide-open frontier town of Dodge City, Kansas, where he signed on as a cowhand. For the next 20 years, he rode the cattle trails, performing feats of skill and strength and getting into numerous scrapes; he later claimed that he had survived 14 separate bullet wounds. In 1890, when the

Nat Love, posing here with the tools of his trade, was a legendary African-American cowboy who rode the cattle range in the years following the Civil War.

railroads finally pushed the cowboys off the plains, Love began a second career as a Pullman porter, wrote his memoirs, and settled into a peaceful and prosperous life in California with his wife and children.

47

Chapter 5 | FORGE AND FURNACE

A woodcut of African blacksmiths at work. In many parts of West Africa, blacksmiths are admired for their skill but also feared as potentially dangerous magicians. For this reason, they have often been obliged to live apart from the rest of the community.

Before the Iron Age, Africans lived as hunter-gatherers, moving from place to place in small bands of fewer than 30 people. Only when they learned to make iron axes and hoes could Africans clear large portions of land and plant enough crops to live in permanent communities. As these communities grew, the possession of iron swords and iron-tipped spears and arrows enabled ambitious warrior groups to conquer peoples who were equipped only with weapons made of stone and bone. These conquests led directly to the founding of Africa's great kingdoms and empires.

Africans began to smelt iron about 2,500 years ago. They heated chunks of rock under high temperatures in charcoal-fired clay furnaces to extract the iron ore (known as the bloom), which could then be heated at a blacksmith's forge and fashioned into various tools and weapons. Though the craft of making iron may have originated with the Phoenicians in the Middle East, Africans soon demonstrated great skill and innovation. As early as 1,500 years ago, Africans in present-day Tanzania began inserting the *tuyère* (the pipe that feeds air into the furnace) deeper into the combustion chamber. As a result, the temperature in the furnace rose so high that some of the charcoal's carbon crystals adhered to the iron. The addition of carbon created steel, a form of iron that was stronger and more durable than standard wrought iron. European iron manufacturers did not match this technology until the 19th century.

What Europeans lacked in tech-

Nineteenth-century African warriors fashioning iron weapons. Many of the ancient African kingdoms were founded by warrior groups whose possession of iron lances, swords, and arrowheads enabled them to conquer neighbors equipped with weapons of stone and animal bones.

nique, however, they made up for in volume of production. Sometime after the 14th century, Europeans began to use a water-powered wheel to pump the bellows that sent air into the furnace, raising the temperature enough to produce iron that was easier to mold (though not as strong as steel). The European blast furnace, essentially a tall brick chimney rising about 20 feet from the ground, could also operate continually for months at a time; the end result was more iron with less labor.

When they began settling in the Americas, Europeans built furnaces and forges wherever they could find waterways with enough flow to power the wheels. The manufacture of iron for items such as plows, axe heads, cooking utensils, wheel rims, and wagon axles was essential to the growth of the New World economy. In the southern United States, especially, this production depended on a combination of European and African talents.

Iron making required a skilled and reliable work force, and from the earliest days southern iron manufacturers found free white laborers unsatisfactory. William Weaver, who entered the iron business in western Virginia during the early 19th century, wrote to an associate that white laborers were extremely poor workmen. Weaver also observed that in "moments of the greatest pressure & necessity, the proprietor must either make them advances which they will never repay, or they leave his service to the ruin of his business." Thus, the vast majority of ironworkers throughout Virginia, Kentucky, and Tennessee were Africans and African Americans. Some were purchased outright by the iron makers, but most were hired on a yearly basis from the owners of plantations.

Africans may have been able to adapt to specialized tasks such as those involved in ironwork because they had developed complex divisions of labor in their own countries. Almost all the leading African monarchs had created hereditary guilds of craftsmen who lived in the royal capital, each assigned to its own quarter of the city. These guilds were closed to outsiders, and in many nations the craftspeople worked exclusively for the royal court. Outside the capital, each major village had at least one blacksmith, whose iron-making skills were regarded with a mixture of awe and fear.

In addition to their work at the furnace and forge, slaves at ironworks performed other essential tasks. They

52

quarried stone to erect the furnaces and other buildings; cut and hauled timber for the charcoal that fueled the furnaces; built dams to regulate water power; and grew the crops needed to feed their families. Though the work was hard and sometimes dangerous, many black iron-workers enjoyed advantages unknown to the average plantation slave.

Because the quality of the product depended so much on the skill of the workers—especially the master refiner and the operators of the great trip-ham-mer that shaped the heated iron—iron manufacturers often provided incentives for able slaves. Work was organized on the task system, and those who had filled their production quota were paid for any extra work they produced. As a result of this "overwork," a number of slaves were able to afford small luxuries and build up savings accounts. In addi-tion, the workers often found that they could, within reason, dictate their own pace. When they felt the need for extra time off, they could simply remain at home and send word that they were ill. The master might be annoyed and grumble about "slacking," but he could hardly afford to fire any of his skilled workers over such a minor issue. Not surprisingly, some plantation owners were reluctant to hire out their slaves to iron foundries: one who did so com-plained that his slaves had "got a habit of roaming about and *taking care of themselves.*"

Whatever advantages they pos-sessed, however, black ironworkers were free to "roam about" only in a limited sense. They were still slaves who lacked the freedom to change their place of res-idence or change jobs if a better oppor-tunity came along. Though many took pride in their skill, their status kept them from improving still further and also prevented the South's iron industry from keeping pace with developments in the more prosperous North. One foundry operator lamented in 1812 that his slaves "were as good workmen 20 years ago as they are now—they have had no chance to improve—they have not an opportunity of travelling to see other works and the annual improve-ments. . . . The father and son joggs on in the old way."

Black ironworkers in the cities, some slave and some free, were better able to

African-American riveters employed in a southern shipyard pose for a photo in 1918. In the years following the Civil War, African-American workers excelled in fields such as mining, steelwork, ship-building, and railway construction.

54

escape these limitations. The remarkable ornamental ironworks—balconies, lamp brackets, and other architectural features—that survive in New Orleans and in a number of Brazilian cities were the work of black craftsmen. Some scholars have argued that these creations were a direct transference of African skills, pointing to the exquisite metalwork done through the centuries by artists in Yorubaland, Igboland, Dahomey, and Benin. Others believe that purely African design concepts were lost in the New World and replaced by a distinctively African-American style. In either case, the work itself testifies to the skill and imagination of those early generations of black artisans. Their contribution to the building of cities, towns, factories, and railroads is indicated by their numbers: at the end of the Civil War in 1865, there were 100,000 black artisans in the South, compared to only 20,000 whites with similar skills.

When the slaves became free laborers after the Civil War, they played a major role in the Reconstruction Era, which lasted from 1865 to 1877. During this period, black workers formed their own organizations, such as the Longshoremen's Protective Association of South Carolina, which had 800 members and engaged in a number of successful strikes. For the first time, African Americans were able to serve in state legislatures throughout the South, and these men led the way in efforts to rebuild industries and erect public institutions such as hospitals and schools.

When the federal government withdrew its support for Reconstruction, southern whites systematically excluded African Americans from political life and stripped them of the legal rights they had gained through postwar legislation. Not surprisingly, these southerners were also eager to deny the extent to which African Americans had contributed to the development of the South and the rest of the nation. This new onslaught of falsification and injustice did not begin to abate until the rise of the civil rights movement in the 1950s. Just as scholars began to explore the rich history of Africa and understand its vast empires and accomplishments, so too did the extensive contributions of African Americans to the building of this nation now begin to be recognized.

The colonization of the Americas was ultimately, in the words of Latin American historian Frank Tannenbaum, a "joint Afro-European enterprise"—even though one partner joined the endeavor under compulsion. Without European expansionism, initiative, and ruthlessness, millions of Africans would probably never have migrated to the New World. By the same token, Europeans could probably never have realized their colonial ambitions without the skills and forced labor of millions of Africans. At best, many now-populous areas in North and South America would have remained undeveloped for a long time, and the history of the entire world would have been decidedly different.

55

CHRONOLOGY

1460s	Portuguese mariners begin trade relations with various kingdoms along Africa's Atlantic coast
1470s	Export of African slaves to Europe flourishes
1492	Christopher Columbus lands on Hispaniola in the Caribbean Sea, beginning the era of European expansion into the Americas
1498	First enslaved African reaches the Americas, accompanying Columbus on his third voyage of exploration
1513	African slaves take part in Balboa's journey across the isthmus of Panama to the Pacific Ocean
1517	Spanish make first major shipment of African slaves to the Caribbean islands
1520	African slaves take part in Francisco Pizzaro's conquest of Peru
1542	Spanish monarchy outlaws enslavement of Indians in the Americas; African slave trade increases in volume
1619	First African slaves are brought to the American colonies
c. 1660-85	Britain, France, and the Netherlands replace Spain as the dominant colonial powers in the Caribbean and assume control of the slave trade
c. 1670	African slaves spearhead boat-building and cattle-raising industries in South Carolina; runaway slaves create the kingdom of Palmares in eastern Brazil

1694	Portuguese authorities destroy the kingdom of Palmares
c. 1700	Sugar produced by slave labor in the Americas becomes the most valuable commodity on the world market and spurs the rise of factories in Europe; African slaves begin to cultivate rice in South Carolina
c. 1800	Cotton replaces sugar as the major commodity on the world market; cotton cultivation begins to dominate the slave economy of the southern United States
1807-8	British and U.S. governments outlaw the transatlantic slave trade, though an illegal trade continues for many years
1810	Slave population in the United States reaches one million
1815	France abolishes the importation of slaves to its Caribbean possessions
1850	Slave population in the United States increases to four million
1865	Thirteenth Amendment to the Constitution abolishes slavery throughout the United States; Brazil remains the only American nation with legalized slavery
1865-77	Reconstruction period in United States; African Americans gain legal rights and participate in the political life of the nation
1866-85	5,000 black cowboys help drive cattle herds along the Chisholm Trail; African-American cavalry troops play major role in the settlement of the western frontier
1885	Slavery is abolished in Brazil; transatlantic slave trade officially ends

FURTHER READING

Ball, Charles. *Fifty Years in Chains, or, the Life of an American Slave.* 1837. Detroit: Negro History Press, 1969.

Berlin, Ira, and Philip D. Morgan, eds. *Cultivation and Culture: Labor and the Shaping of Slave Life in the Americas.* Charlottesville: University Press of Virginia, 1993.

Craton, Michael. *Searching for the Invisible Man: Slaves and Plantation Life in Jamaica.* Cambridge: Harvard University Press, 1978.

Davidson, Basil. *The African Slave Trade.* Rev. ed. Boston: Little, Brown, 1980.

Dew, Charles B. *Bond of Iron: Master and Slave at Buffalo Forge.* New York: Norton, 1994.

Equiano, Olaudah. *Equiano's Travels.* Edited by Paul Edwards. London: Heinemann, 1967.

Genovese, Eugene D. *Roll, Jordan, Roll: The World the Slaves Made.* New York: Vintage, 1976.

——. *The Political Economy of Slavery.* 2nd ed. Middletown, CT: Wesleyan University Press, 1989.

Harris, J. E. "The African Diaspora in the Old and New Worlds." In *UNESCO General History of Africa,* vol 5. Berkeley: University of California Press, 1992.

Love, Nat. *The Life and Adventures of Nat Love.* New York: Arno Press/New York Times, 1968.

Mattoso, Katia M. de Queirós. *To Be a Slave in Brazil, 1550-1888.* Translated by Arthur Goldhammer. New Brunswick, NJ: Rutgers University Press, 1986.

Olmsted, Frederick Law. *The Cotton Kingdom: A Traveller's Observations on Cotton and Slavery in the American Slave States.* 1861. New York: Knopf, 1962.

Park, Mungo. *Travels in the Interior Districts of Africa.* 1799. New York: Arno Press/New York Times, 1971.

Pescatello, Ann M., ed. *The African in Latin America.* New York: Knopf, 1975.

Phillips, Ulrich B. *American Negro Slavery.* New York: Appleton, 1918.

Rose, Wille Lee, ed. *A Documentary History of Slavery in North America.* New York: Oxford University Press, 1976.

Stampp, Kenneth. *The Peculiar Institution: Slavery in the Ante-Bellum South.* New York: Vintage, 1956.

Tannenbaum, Frank. *Slave and Citizen.* 1947. Boston: Beacon, 1992.

Thornton, John. *Africa and Africans in the Making of the Atlantic World, 1400-1680.* Cambridge: Cambridge University Press, 1992.

Van Sertima, Ivan. "African Presence in Early America." In Hyatt, Vera Lawrence, and Rex Nettleford, eds. *Race, Discourse, and the Origin of the Americas.* Washington, DC: Smithsonian Institution Press, 1995.

Vernon, Amelia Watson. *African Americans at Mars Bluff, South Carolina.* Baton Rouge: Louisiana State University Press, 1993.

Wood, Peter H. *Black Majority: Negroes in Colonial South Carolina from 1670 Through the Stono Rebellion.* New York: Norton, 1975.

GLOSSARY

antebellum
"before the war" in Latin; used to describe the southern United States before the outbreak of the Civil War in 1860

anthropology
the study of human beings with regard to factors such as race, environment, social relations, and culture

blast furnace
a type of furnace, commonly used for the reduction of iron ore, in which burning charcoal is kept at high heat by a continual draft of pressurized air

cotton gin
a machine that separates cotton fibers from the seed of the plant; its invention in 1793 led to the emergence of cotton as the major crop of the American South

dokpwe
a collective work group in the African kingdom of Dahomey

emancipation
the act of freeing an individual or people from bondage; specifically, the liberation of African-American slaves during and after the U.S. Civil War

flail
a long stick used for beating rice stalks in order to harvest the pods

forge
a workshop where wrought iron is heated and hammered into various shapes

gang system
a method of plantation labor in which a job is performed by a body of slaves working in unison for the length of the workday

hogshead
a large barrel traditionally used for shipping commodities such as sugar or tobacco; 63 gallons in capacity according to the standard U.S. measure

hominids	early humanlike creatures that originated in Africa about 7.5 million years ago; the ancestors of modern humans
indentured servant	a resident of the North American colonies who was obliged to serve a master for a fixed number of years before gaining his or her freedom
Iron Age	the period in history, beginning about 500 B.C. in Africa, marked by the working of iron into tools and weapons
overwork	system by which slaves were allowed to earn money by performing labor that exceeded an assigned task
plantation	an estate devoted to large-scale agriculture
Reconstruction	the period of U.S. history extending from 1865 to 1877, when emancipated African Americans obtained legal and political rights
savanna	landscape featuring rolling grasslands and open woodlands; common to the central regions of West Africa
task system	a method of plantation labor in which each slave is assigned a specific amount of work and is free to leave the field after reaching his or her quota
transatlantic slave trade	traffic in human beings that lasted roughly from 1450 to 1870 and resulted in the migration of at least 12 million Africans to the Americas
Triangle Trade	the 18th-century economic system linking European factories, the African slave trade, and the sugar plantations of the Caribbean
tuyére	a tube through which air is pumped into the combustion chamber of a blast furnace

INDEX

PHILIP KOSLOW earned his B.A. and M.A. degrees from New York University and went on to teach and conduct research at Oxford University, where his interest in medieval European and African history was awakened. In addition to writing the preceding 11 volumes of THE KINGDOMS OF AFRICA, he is the author of *El Cid* in the Chelsea House series HISPANICS OF ACHIEVEMENT and of *Centuries of Greatness: The West African Kingdoms, 750-1900* in Chelsea House's MILESTONES IN BLACK AMERICAN HISTORY series.

PICTURE CREDITS

page

2: Corbis-Bettmann
6: Illustration by Sandra L. Taccone
8-9: Library of Congress, #62-106828
10: Schomburg Center For Research In Black Culture, NYPL
12: Art Resource
15: Art Resource

Color Section
17: Werner Forman Archive Museum of Art, Dallas
18: Bridgeman/Art Resource, NY
19: Aldo Tutino/Art Resource, NY

20: Werner Forman Archive National Museum, Lagos

22: General Research Division, NYPL, Astor, Lenox and Tilden Foundation
24: Giraudon/Art Resource, NY
27: The Bettmann Archive
29: Lauros-Giraudon/Art Resource, NY
30: Bibliotheque Nationale, Paris
32: Corbis-Bettmann
34: South Carolina State Museum, Columbia, SC
35: Corbis-Bettmann

Color Section
37: The Pierpont Morgan Library/Art Resource, NY
38: Giraudon/Art Resource, NY
39: Bridgeman/Art Resource, NY
40: Art Resource

42: New York Public Library
44: United Nations
46: The Bettmann Archive
47: Schomburg Center For Research In Black Culture, NYPL
48: Corbis-Bettmann
50: Corbis-Bettmann
53: The Bettmann Archive